But we have this treasure in jars of clay to show that this
all-surpassing power is from God and not from us…

2 Corinthians 4:7

Dedicated to my Wife Janice and Beryl my Mother.

CONTENTS

INTRODUCTION

What have I done! At the risk of sounding glib I literally took the plunge with this project, and it has just grown. And how it has grown! I never in my wildest dreams thought that my writing was good enough to be published. With a lot of encouragement from my publishers 'Daisa Publishing' I have written a number of poems and a short story. A lot of these poems have been with me for a long time and it was an intrepid moment, one night, handing them over to someone who has lots of experience of reading manuscripts. I expected nothing less than a rejection letter, better luck next time, but to my surprise the opposite happened, and I was asked if I had any more!

I am married with two grown up sons who live happily with their partners. I retired at the time of writing this after forty-three years working on the railway in various guises from a driver to working in a number of booking offices. In-between reading and playing snooker I occasionally write the odd poem when I get inspiration. I am a regular member of our congregation at 'St Nicholas Church' in Great Coates, Grimsby and have recently become a Lay Minister within the Church. As you might gather by the subject matter, my Anglican faith is paramount in my life.

I have not had any formal training in writing poetry or short stories of any kind, apart from attending an A level course in English Literature when I was about 30. I got an F which I thought stood for fail, until recently.

Most of this book has been writing from the heart, life experiences, shouting at the tv when events happen that have been frustrating. All written initially in a matter of minutes and most of the poems have not had much revision, so they are here exactly as I wrote them.

I hope they give you pleasure, inspiration, comfort or whatever you see in them. The short story was taken from a postcard depicting a Ukrainian woman picking up firewood that I was given for homework when I was doing my A level. I hope you like it. Not every poem will find favour with everyone. But if a couple make your heart flutter, or the hairs on the back of your neck tingle, or even if they make you think, then my job is done!

Enjoy and God be with you.

Mark Sandford

FIGHT THE GOOD FIGHT

Fight the good fight
With all of your might!
Put on your breastplate and shield
Then follow, come hither
Down to the river.
The water runs deep and will heal.
Put down those fears.
Love lingers here
Take up your cross and leave
Then you will see
All you can be
Come, soldier of Love and just Breathe!

THANK YOU FOR THE RAIN

In England's scorched savannah
Where grass and sage die out,
Where withered trees like gnarled Acacia
Stand like sentries, waiting for rain.

Like antelope and zebra on sun drenched plain
We wait in the drought for life quenching rain!
A sprinkling, a splash, then, with whispered refrain
Heat rises with vigour, and once again
We wait for the rain.

So Africa shines on Jerusalem's shore,
But when the rain comes, it will pour and pour!

CLEAN WHITE SHEETS

And so, with trembling heart
I dare to embrace your clean white sheet
And mark it with my scribblings.
To make a sentence, where to start?
And where to feel complete?
Does it matter if my style don't rhyme?
I'm sure that it will come,
Given time.

And so, with trembling heart
I start to make my mark on clean white sheets
And fall apart…

FROGS!

We sit like frogs around the swamp
To contemplate our sin.
And croak our brutally realistic din
At all who wait for Him!
Proclaiming loud to those who wait
For hope to come so free.
And somehow speak of what may be
If only we believe!
To all those folk who pray in hope,
I make this wholesome plea
Just close your eyes and truly pray;
The wonderful Lord will come.
His Light shines bright, not just for some,
But for all loud croaking frogs, today!

THANK YOU

How the years pass!
With sweet innocence gone
To the mists of time;
A memory, a smell, like new mown grass;
All in a moment, long gone!
Places familiar, sounds too.
Each grain of sand drops with lament,
But You Lord
Are there to guide me on.
Some new thoughts, mingled with old,
With new experiences too to unfold.
I'm living life to the full,
Knowing, soon you will call,
So I thank you, Lord, for it all!

OPEN EYES

With eyes wide open
And with faith so true
I show my thanks in all I do;
Because I put my faith in you.

With eyes wide open
Here's my love for you,
Because you're here; in everything
It's you.

My eyes wide opened
To the love you give
So that the life that I live
Is devoted to you;

And the prayers that are said
In the stillness of time,
Will be spoken in truth,
For the truth I will find,
Because I've opened my eyes

To your Love!

ENGLISH ROSE

A simple rose by any other name!
It's innocence and beauty is profound!
It sits there in protective gown, underground,
Fed and watered by rain and sun.
Yet you do not know what you have done!
Surely this English Rose is not to blame!
It must be some other tree.
Those barbs on our English species
Cannot perpetrator be!
The one whose spines adorn Him.
See; they're not the same.
Or could it be?
Could they be some import from the Roman tree?
That came from English soil so fair
And fashioned in that gruesome crown
In barbaric majesty!
It bares not thought to look at one
So full of radiant beauty
Hauntingly has turned, I weep,
Of hurting…
But with resolute and graceful plea!

IF NOT GOD

In constant love of life
In perfect peace or strife.
In feeling whole or alone.
In all that's done or undone.
If not God, then who?

In feeling hurt or in grief
In all that comes with belief.
In all to care for with love
In all that comes from above.
If not God, then who?

CALVARY

I look at you!
Squatting here on this filthy hill
your arms outstretched on your tree
Crying out to our God above!
Eye to eye, we dare to see;
Me with guilt, You with aching love!

I look at you…
And find my thoughts turn
To this thing we have done?
Your spirit, Three in one
Has been forsaken and gone.
Yet your light shines on
In the darkness like a beacon

I look at you…
And think of my denial
When at your trial
You needed me most
But I ran through the streets
As the cockerel crowed
With your face lingering on, like a ghost
Through the loving tears that flowed.

I look at you…
So innocent a child
Soon to be defiled.

But for now in the frost and the cold
Peaceful and warm
On your mother's arm
In a stable as the scriptures foretold.

YOUNG BOY

Could I have as much faith as him
Who lies with waxen skin, so frail?
His arms so thin, I'd fear they'll break:
Eyes wide, pleading still, pales
Insignificant to those who wail
And plead for food!
Paraded now for all to ponder,
Is his faith still whole, I wonder?
Who would blame him years to come?
If God is not his wholesome fan!
For life is on the threshold here
And other things are here to fear!
I'm trying to replicate if I can
How I would feel!
Of course I can't!
But God is here, this I know
You see his mother's eyes
Where love is strong and tears they flow
As they peer up heavenward to the skies.
And now I surely know
His faith is pure and sound!
For God is working here,
Just look around!

SMITHEREENS

In the smoke and smithereens;
Bodies broke, bloody and sheen
Weighed down with mortar, blind, unseen
And still it comes those smithereens.

Innocent child fresh of mind
and all of clean;
No political lips foreseen
Or voices sounding thoughts unclean!
Yet still they come, these smithereens!

Stop!
Just stop this venting spleens
Of bombing people to smithereens
Peace must prevail!
God has seen that which all has been
And will renounce all sinful fiends!

But still, here comes more Smithereens!

NO COST

I can almost bear this torment
Knowing you are near.
This harried, torrid lament
If you are but here
To shine a shaft of light
Through this shroud of darkness:
This pain that lingers in the heart
And turns and mixes all it festers.
And you know everything my lord:
Every single twist and turn.
And even though I feel you're here
The one thing that is constant Lord
Is fear.
So help me through this troubled mind
This feeling of remorse and loss.
And soon I know that I will find
There is all conquering love, no cost.

GOING 'HOME'

A short story

He dare not move!

His heart was beating fast as he tried to hide behind the tree. After getting this far, he was going to be found out and taken back to the trenches. Where could he go?

The old woman was collecting sticks and twigs as she stooped to the ground which was strewn with dead leaves from the trees. The wood had given him good coverage to escape - or so he thought. But he watched the old woman for a long time.

The light was fading fast as day turned to dusk and the grey sky seemed to get heavier as the September mist shrouded the woods. Strange too to notice that the rifle cracks and shells that droned overhead all day when he was in the trenches had gone silent.

He squatted behind the beech tree as the old woman came closer. She was humming a little tune to herself as she collected her wood. A little dog by her side sniffed the ground and made the obligatory scent mark on various tree trunks.

"You wouldn't mind helping an old woman collect firewood now would you? It's getting dark and I've left a nice pot of rabbit stew on the go. Come out where I can see you!"

The shock of her voice now echoing around the woods startled him and made him make gestures at her.

"Keep the voice down! Someone will hear you. I'm toast if they catch me."

At the sound of his voice the dog started to bark, and it took him all his nerves of steel not to go up to the dog and cut its throat with his knife, but then he suddenly remembered, he'd lost it somewhere in the wood.

"Oh your secret is safe with me young man. It's fine, no one can hear us, come out and help. As I say I've a nice pot of stew on the stove and you look like you haven't eaten for some considerable time."

And so hesitantly he revealed himself and walked towards the old woman and started helping her pick up sticks. Eventually, she decided she had enough wood and with a little sing-song command to the dog, she turned around and started walking in the direction she had come from.

The deserter followed, not knowing why, but couldn't understand how an old woman could be living in a house somewhere in the middle of a wood, right in the cross-fire of a war zone.

It was 1916 somewhere in Belgium and the war had become a stalemate between the two warring factions. The Deserter had had enough and had been planning his escape for months.

In a clearing stood a little cottage, like something you would imagine out of a story book. White walls, and candlelight flickering through the windows. A wisp of smoke came out of the chimney and as the weary travellers got closer they could smell woodsmoke.

Pheasants and rabbits hung on hooks from the walls which looked like they had recently been killed.

"What's your name then young man? I can't have you sat at my table eating my food without you telling me that at least"

"Herbert, Herbert Whitfield Ma'am"

"And how old are you Herbert?" she enquired as she put the wood down on a bench next to the front door.

"Seventeen," he stammered "but I told them I was eighteen when I volunteered to join, so that I could come to fight in this war. I wish I hadn't bothered now"

"We'll come to that soon enough lad. Now take your shoes off and come in out of the cold. Pip! Come on Pip." Obediently, the dog and Herbert followed the old woman into the house.

The house glowed as the fire in the hearth blazed away and the room smelt of the rabbit stew bubbling away on the little black stove. Herbert had never smelt anything so good since he had left home over a year ago, his stomach grumbled in agreement, for he had not eaten much for days.

"There is a small room behind you where you can wash and make yourself a little presentable, go and clean up while I prepare supper," she instructed as she promptly took off her shawl.

She looked to be well in her eighties with silver grey hair that finished in a small bun at the back of her head. Well-worn hands that looked like she had done many years of labour quickly laid two places at the wooden table for supper. Her face was etched with Crow's feet at the corner of keen eyes that seemed to be as clear as blue water and were hypnotising to anyone who cared to stare into them. She had a mana of Aurora about her that commanded attention whenever she spoke.

Strangely there did not seem to be any remnants of utensils for the preparation of the meal she had evidently cooked, but fresh bread and wine was provided as well as rabbit stew.

A spinning Jenny rested in one of the corners of the room and that seemed to be the most intricate piece of furniture that was installed. Simple chairs and a wooden table, sink and worktable all in one room, with a smaller room off to one side, presumably with a bed etc.

Herbert emerged from that room a little later, refreshed and looking a little cleaner than when they first met each other.

"Now sit yourself down young man, I hope you like rabbit stew," she said as she prepared to serve Herbert a large bowl of the piping hot broth.

As she sat down herself, she promptly closed her eyes, put her palms together and prayed for the meal.

Herbert watched her intently and turned his eyes away as she caught him staring.

"Don't you believe in God, Mr Whitfield?"

"Herbert, call me Herbert. I... I did," he stammered. "But not anymore."

"You must have faith boy! Jesus died on the cross for all mankind, even those in times of war. Don't get downhearted, eat your stew before it goes cold," she chided.

Herbert ate greedily, pulling apart great wedges of bread to soak up all the tasty gravy in his bowl.

"Tell me Herbert, why did you leave your post? The trenches are a horrible place, I know, but you must have had a very good reason to run. Some people have been shot for deserting their post you know. Not that I advocate that mind, as I abhor all kinds of violence."

Herbert looked at her, midway through a mouthful of bread, in thought, struggling with himself whether to confide in this stranger. He decided that it would be an insult to the old woman's hospitality to not tell her and so he blurted out his reason.

"I have a sweetheart at home. We were going to marry one day and I figured that to do that I had to survive. Sitting in those trenches, you don't know what it was like Ma'am. The stench and stink of fear, broken men, older than me who couldn't perform anymore, shaking with shell shock. Body parts strewn around no-man's land; it was awful. My mate who I went to school with was shot in the head. I cried all night, I had to get away." He was becoming delirious with the thought of recounting his horror, and the old woman had to sooth his fears and bring him back down from the brink of war.

"Shh," she soothed, "it's all over now. You won't ever need to go back there again, I promise."

"You won't take me back?" he asked with a little panic in his voice.

"No," she said. "You won't be going back there, but I can assure you that you will be going *home* soon, once you have faith."

"Faith?" he questioned, "faith in what?"

"Faith in the Lord, my child. Now drink up, its getting late," and she threw a scrap of bread to Pip the dog, who had been sitting patiently by her side.

Herbert wondered what she was talking about, all this faith in the Lord business, it wasn't natural, unless you were some kind of religious freak, but he decided to go along.

"Tell me how I need to have faith in the Lord then Miss."

"Pray!" she shouted, which startled Herbert, and the dog.

"Pray with all your heart and all your soul and all your mind. Love the Lord as He loves you always," she exclaimed.

"I do, I do," Herbert said. "It's just that right now I'm having a bit of trouble having faith when all that death and destruction is around," he said gesturing outside with his hand.

"Forget that and pray with me!" The old woman said enthusiastically.

Herbert started feeling frightened for the first time since they had met. It was the most time he had seen the old woman so animated. She poured another glass of wine for them both and said, "aren't you feeling sleepy yet?"

"Actually, I am feeling a bit tired yes."

"Well let's drink to you and Charlotte getting married soon and then we'll call it a night!"

Herbert's heart missed a beat.

"How do you know my *Charlottes* name? Are you some sort of spy, you said you weren't going to take me back!"

"Do I look like a spy lad?" she retorted.

"Relax, as I said, your secret is safe with me, I know lots of things, but you mustn't worry about that. Trust me you will see Charlotte soon. You'll be going home; wouldn't you like to do that?"

"Stop playing games with me," Herbert said, feeling quite frightened now, but also his eyelids were starting to feel very heavy too.

"Drink up and let's get you to bed, you look very tired. Perhaps it's the wine going to your head a little," as she helped him towards the room, where the bed had been made.

"Let's say the Lord's Prayer before we retire," she insisted.

But Herbert got to the third line of the prayer and fell asleep.

Morning came with a bang! Shells were whizzing overhead and the sound of gunfire rattled around the trees. Some trees were pulverised by the latest shell smashing into them.

Herbert woke with a start.

He was naked! Looking around him, he saw that the bed had gone! In-fact the house and the old woman had gone too!

Herbert stood up shivering to put his clothes on, looking frantically around him.

Was it all a dream?

Was he delirious?

Anther shell whizzed over-head and he was just deciding which way to run when he heard voices.

Frightened and anxious to get away he fled in the opposite direction and stepped on a land mine...

WALNUT INK

And now my life-blood set free:
From seedlings earthbound to the tree.
To protective casing, opened up
To reveal my body, trapped, now see
How I mark this parchment, permanently.
Earthly hue
From old to new.
Precious, palpable, pleasant but
So versatile, this ancient nut.

STAR

I saw the star for the first time tonight;
It came as a gift so bright in flight,
This star of mine.
And this night felt so right.

I saw the babe for the first time tonight,
Wrapped in wool to keep him warm.
And I knew somehow that my life this night
Was his reason to be born!

And the star shone so bright and so new;
For all the world, for me and for you

Let it shine forever!

GETHSENEME

I should have stayed this night!
This night, when you needed me most.
This night when the darkness comes
Bringing fear and rejection!
And like everyone here, I ran.
Even now, on this night.
Simon Peter ran! Even Andrew and John!
On this night, Your Son was alone!
And we fled in our fear and our tears
To our warm safe homes
On this night!
When the moon smiled down as it shone.
Then the soldiers came, on this night,
And took Him away to be scorned
And ridiculed, scourged and beaten
On this night!
And the cock crowed
In the break of the morn
As we denied Him thrice
And ran, on this night…
… And every year for two thousand years we have ran
On this night!
Back to our safe warm homes!
And we leave you there with the candlelight

And pray for the end of this night.
For Salvation comes in the morning
In the light of the glorious cross!
Until next year, when we run with fear
In the night, with our silence and loss...

HEARING AIDS

It sure is hard when hearing fails
When all the world is shades of grey
When even babes have lost their wail
And nothing matches what folk say.

Take asking for a railway plan
To somewhere south and back again
The traveller returns by the same route
And all you hear is by Beruit!
It's such a shame and what does pain
When folk have asked for railcard wallets
And all you hear is they want a wallop!

And the guy who has asked for the toilet keys
And I've given him a return ticket to Leeds!
No my friends it's not so good
When hearing goes, it's clear as mud
And music, life and good things fade.
Although I'm wearing hearing aids!

What?

RAINBOW

There's a rainbow riding high
A splash of colour in the sky.
But if you squint and scrunch your eyes
What do you see?

A chariot flashing by,
Rising to the top then fly
Down the other side
In valiant cry
Of valour!

Or Unicorns, their spiralled horns
Rising to the misty morn
The sun rising high a new day born
In summer

And if you really are so bold
All manner of things behold.
Let your mind indulge; you're sold
For not all things will turn to gold!

WHITE HELMETS

In the dust and rubble, through fire and mortar
In the background, war-torn Syria, bangs and rotors.
Apparitions tend to the sick and dying.
White helmets not for the want of trying
Save the children of this land!

I pray for their courage!
As I sit here in my comfortable chair
And scribble thoughts down on paper,
Some charitable person saves life and limb,
And only they seem to care.

But now we hear they are in danger,
Some politic has declared.
Is it wrong to do God's work
In the land so close to the Manger?
Are we so happy to shirk our responses
While death becomes a thing uncared?

Save them yes, and keep them safe,
But save the land from whence they came!
Give peace a chance, we all should pray.
Their work puts us all to shame.

THE EASY

Why is the easy so difficult to master?
Would our mind be any wiser
Or our love grow any faster
If our love for Him was made so hard?
Would our struggles and our fight
For power, might and greed
Constrict our desire to be free?
So that the darkness snuffs out the light.
And we make our lives so difficult,
So complicated, hard to see that
The easy thing is always to be
In grace, in peace and most definitely
In Love.

That's not so difficult, says He…

SYRIA

When we last met in rubble and stress
I scarcely knew myself, for fear was all around me.
Nothing here was blessed.
A shaft of light appeared; so bright I could not see;
And peace was all around: no bombs, no guns, just me.

You held out a hand, so warm, so free
That none could resist its pull,
My fear just up and went from me,
That beckoning hand, so full
Of love was very hard to see-

Because through tears; so faithfully
In streets of blood, of shame,
A man as you would seek me out:
You never portioned blame.

In deathly silence, out I came
From that infernal flame.
Your peace, and love was all around.
Jesus was your name…

THE PIANIST

Hands that float across Ivory
Tinkle in such ecstasy
To stir my soul, to soar on high;
my heart it reaches out to fly
On every note that plays
With emotion frayed.
So broken with sound
Until tears of love are dripping,
Drowned; around this sacred soul.
Those fingers mesmerise with speed,
The hungry soul it feeds:
Wet, with emotion now I find
The inner self has awoken my mind
With the sound, so powerful and strong.

Spent, his power lingers long…

CHUMS

In some distant poppied Clag,
Furled, in some weathered union flag,
Lay the future of our world.
A century of clashes, hurled!
Innocent, and bold, and seventeen
Amongst his personals; watch, canteen.
White with fear; so long unseen!
With songs of hope and glory
Charging through gassed fog:
Now, his melancholy story
Whispered from the bog.
One hundred years!
One million tears!
Forgotten chums laid out like ghosts
As the bugler's song plays their last post.

EPILOGUE

Charlotte sat restless in her wheelchair feeling the cold November air on her chest as the World War One centenary commemorations got under way. She was 118 years old and still going strong, or so her great granddaughter had been telling everyone.

Most people who were around when the first world war, known as the 'Great War' had happened, were decidedly deceased. But there were one or two left, like Charlotte still around to tell the tale.

She had come all this way to Amiens to pay tribute to her brother, who had been shot in the head during one of the great battles in the trenches in the area. Rebecca, her great granddaughter had paid for her passage to the war graves here, as it would probably be the last time Charlotte would have been able to come.

Charlotte was already plagued with a few illnesses and she had always been wanting to come to Amiens but was never able to in the past. So here they were after the ceremonies had finished, taking in the ambience of the event.

A watery sun shone down on them as Charlotte sat restless and tearful next to a bench where Rebecca sat.

They had been to visit Bobby, but there was another person there that Charlotte was keen to see. His name was Herbert Whitfield.

"The graves are in alphabetical order, Rebecca, can you take me to the W's please."

Rebecca dutifully took her great grandma down the line of graves that started with W's and they went down the lines. Watson to Wick and Whig until they reached Whitfield, and there he was…

"Who was he, Great Grandma?" Rebecca inquired.

"That, young girl was my Herbert, my sweet Herbie. We were to be married you know, oh yes, but my Father wouldn't let us. You're too young he would say, even when we said we would wait until after the war."

"What was he like, Great Grandma?" Rebecca asked.

"Oh he was charming, handsome and kind. We were at school together. I remember when he used to come on his rickety old bicycle with that wicker basket on the front delivering the bread to Father's shop. That's how we got to know each other. Oh they were happy days. And then we found out that he was mysteriously killed, somewhere around here I expect."

Charlotte lapsed into her memories.

The trees rustled in the breeze as a few more leaves escaped from their branches and floated down on to tombstones. In the distance a lady was humming and you could hear a dog barking.

Rebecca left her great grandmother to her memories and promptly went to find out where the dog was, as she was sure that dogs weren't allowed in the cemetery. As she walked towards the humming of the lady, she hid behind a tree and watched furtively.

The old woman was picking up sticks, and the dog gave out the occasional yelp.

Rebecca couldn't wait any longer.

"Excuse me," she said, revealing herself from behind the tree.

"I don't think dogs are allowed in here," as she glanced back to make sure great grandma was still safe.

"Oh! You gave me a start there young lady, I didn't know you were there. You wouldn't mind helping an old lady pick up some sticks would you?"

"Erm, I don't know," Rebecca stammered as she once again turned to see if Charlotte was ok.

But she wasn't there!

Her great grandma along with the wheelchair had disappeared…

STILL

Take it! Take it all.
For I am open to your Word.
I feel your infinite love come in
Every time I'm purged!
Take my life, and make it yours
To do what you will, I'm still
The man I was, with flaws.
Like a bird, with a preening will,
Searching out that ruffled quill.
For if you set me free
I wouldn't fly.
No I wouldn't fly
And indeed I wouldn't try.
For I know that you love me
Still.

THE SPIRIT

As the inevitable march towards the end
Embraces all my thinking
And my fears become more enhanced
I'm drawn to safer keeping
In the knowledge that your spirit lingers
In the most inviting way.
For as I notice little changes
In the seasons of life,
Winter comes with trepidation.

My fears evaporate on the ether
As I sense you being here.
The trees shimmer with delight
On the whisper of warm respite
And the age old circle of life
Is once again reborn.

So I marvel at the magic of you.
That faithful Holy Spirit
fills my soul with love so true
Something so exquisite!

THORN

I cannot bare to see it now!
It's symbol so profound.
The Passion we so fondly show
To place your thorny crown!
At Passion-tide with love it grows,
For all things come from you!
This delicate, sense filled, fragrant rose;
So red with heavenly hue!
But when I think of what this is,
What symbol, so forlorn.
To rest on one, that with a kiss
Was forced to wear with scorn.
My prayer to you, o loving Lord
Is look upon my sin!
For *I* should wear this shameful thorn,
And ask for Love from Him!

WALKING WITH POPPY

Thiepval, Ypres, Verdun, Somme,
Even Tiperrary come,
Come and see my lonely home!
See lines of stone;
Laid bone to bone!

Hear the bugle play last post
In the villages, coast to coast.
In the silence; in repost
As Big Ben strikes and you toast

The last of Chums here lying now!
One hundred years: As you bow
And feel the tears as they flow
Down cheeks, so young as then, as now.

Come now, walk me to the shore
As you brave the mist and hoar,
Silent, as your heart so pure
Is broken! Think of love, not war!

AS LONG AS THERE IS YOU

As long as there is you
To guide and pull me through
This day and night in all I do
I pray you love me so
As long as there is you.

As long as there is you
To call me by my name
To walk with me, and renew
This holy tongue of flame.

As long as there is you.

WHEN SILENCE FALLS UPON MY WORLD

When all is still: when silence falls upon my world
And I can almost hear my heartbeat.
When my thoughts all turn and unfurl
And I sit quite still on my seat;
I'm sure I can sense your being here

When my world is turned upside down
And my stomach turns in on itself.
When tears come so hard I could drown
In a pool, on the ground
I'm sure I can sense you here.

When my conscience tells me to carry on
And the logic of it all reveals,
When the truth comes out, it won't be long!
In the silence, I sense
You are here, and it feels

So good, my God, so good.

IN MEMORY OF...

Sitting here so peacefully as the sea rolls on its way
I distinctly remember that feeling, the day
I was plunged into depths of despair.
There was so much anguish, so much to say
When you left me to fend for myself, and repair
All that was life, so much to share in work or in our play.
So, sitting here with my bunch of flowers
In a box, for protection you understand,
I watch the birds on the wind for hours
Although to stay this long I never planned
As the cold has crept into my bones
And my morbid thoughts have left me quite alone.
And I stare at your memorial badge
Wishing all that has been done could be
somehow undone.
And the anguish and pain
Through the sun and the rain, as I sit here
Could be gone, and our love would be here as one.
Cracked and in need of some paint
This bench that I sit on and wait
For your return, in the rain and the cold.
And I'm feeling quite lonely and old.

THE LIGHT

In the darkness shines the light:
It pierces through those fears, and fights
The beat of doubt that pains
This faithful heart.
My soul is quenched when you are here
In warmth, in love,
In Eucharistic prayer.
Chanting Psalms, my life laid bare!

Light the lamp for Him who died,
That he might save my soul tonight.
And if the darkness creeps up now
He shines right through,
In Glorious Light!

IN MEMORY OF... MUM

I shall hold you in my thoughts dear
As I wipe away my tears.
In prayer, I think of you always, Mum
And then I smile as I remember.

So many times you cuffed my head
In jest or out of love.
For my stupidity; for things not said
And things I should have said but forgot.

And then there was the times
when all my world was lost.
And you were there, every time
to wrap me in your love.

So every week in solemn prayer
I think of you and wish you were here.
The candle flame glows bright and true
And I can almost imagine that is you!

With Love!

A poem for All Soul's Day

CHAPEL DEACON

Who put that crease in your soul,
Davies, ready this fine morning
For the staid Chapel where the Book's frown
Sobers the sunlight?
Who taught you to pray
And scheme at once, your eyes
Turning skyward, while your swift mind
Weighs your heifers chances in the next towns
Fair on Thursday?
Are your hearts coals kindled for God?
Or is it burning of your lean cheeks
Because you sit too near that girl's smouldering gaze?
Tell me Davies, for the faint breeze
From Heaven freshens and I roll in it,
Who taught you your deft poise?

R S THOMAS

THOUGHTS AND PRAYERS

For in all that discernment through the minds eye
To kindle the peace; to wounds
You might try to relate
With words in that private prayer.
To some, you would care
With their souls laid bare
And their supplicants made aware!
How goes it with you?
With the word on your back
As you weave and tack
Through life's raging sea?
Are your thoughts with crossed brow,
Or kissed, as you bow
Like the willow, weeping at the world?
For I revel in it, knowing full well, that
You yearn for His favour,
Still…

FLYING SOUTH

Honking and gibbering sounds you hear.
Look up now, and you'll see them there;
Squadrons, filling up the air
Flying South another year.

Farewell, Adieu, Bon chance my friends.
Your presence here comes to an end
As winter comes, the favoured trend
Is flying South, on thermal wends.

Then next year, when springtime turns
When buds and grasses sprout through ferns.
The sound of snow geese will return
Another year, another term!

But until then we say Adios
Mis Amigos emplumados!

I AM AN INSTRUMENT OF LOVE

I am an instrument of peace Lord
A vessel: a clay jar.
Reach deep down and fill me with your word:
Your treasure from afar.

I am an instrument of your love Lord.
A parcel: from the heart
That worships with the sound of love
And surely is that start
Of…
I am…

LORD LET ME SING

When I came here, Lord
And you gave me all your love
I didn't show it, oh no
I hid your holy word
When I came here, Lord
And you showed me the way
I didn't know, oh no Lord
What to say

But now, my loving Lord
The words that I sing
Are from this loving heart
Of mine, and it's a beautiful thing
Because, of the beautiful words
I want to be a part
Of your Love

Yes I do, Lord
Oh I do, Lord
Let me sing…

ALL IS WELL

Love has shed a tear tonight.
Darkness comes, but bright the light.
He closes eyelids, shut them tight
Let sleep dissolve you, through this night
And love will hold you, all is well.
In the morn, when sounds the bell
You'll be here, and you can tell
About His Love

For all is well…

ACKNOWLEDGEMENTS

I would like to take this opportunity to thank a few people, dear friends who have helped make this all possible:

To Daisa Publishing, and especially Daisa and Jade who have had the confidence to say that my work is good enough to be published. I am indebted to everyone who works at Daisa Publishing for believing in me.

To Fr Peter Mullins who always gave me encouragement and read most of these poems and gave constructive criticism.

To Carol Frankish whom I regard as my proof reader and biggest fan, thank you.

To R S Thomas and George Herbert who gave me inspiration and love of poetry

For Reverend Anne for her encouragement and kind words
Lastly, for my Wife Janice, my fiercest critic.

Thank you also to anyone I have not mentioned but should have; they are forever in my prayers and thoughts for giving me encouragement and advice

With Love,
Mark Sandford

BV - #0010 - 160920 - C0 - 198/129/4 - PB - 9781916225169